My Day,
Our World

Written by Charlotte Raby
and Emily Guille-Marrett

Collins

Can you talk about your day?

 After reading

Letters and Sounds: Phase 1

Word count: 0

Curriculum links: Understanding the World: The World

Early Learning Goals: Listening and attention: children listen attentively in a range of situations; Understanding: answer 'how' and 'why' questions about their experiences and in response to stories or events; Reading: demonstrate understanding when talking with others about what they have read

Developing fluency

- Encourage your child to hold the book and to turn the pages.
- Look at the pictures together and encourage your child to talk about what they see, explaining in as much detail as they can.

Phonic practice

- Look at page 4 together. Ask your child if they can find a word in the picture that rhymes with 'map' (tap). Now do the same thing for the following pages:

  page 7: coat (*boat*)

  page 8: toy (*boy*)

  page 13: ted (*bed*)

Extending vocabulary

- Look at pages 6–7 together. Ask your child:

  How many different ways to get to school can you see in these pictures? Can you name them all? Can you think of any other types of transport?

- Ask your child to spot the odd one out in each of the following groups of words:

  o boy   cup   girl   (*cup*)

  o bus   boat   cat   (*cat*)

  o book   skip   run   (*book*)